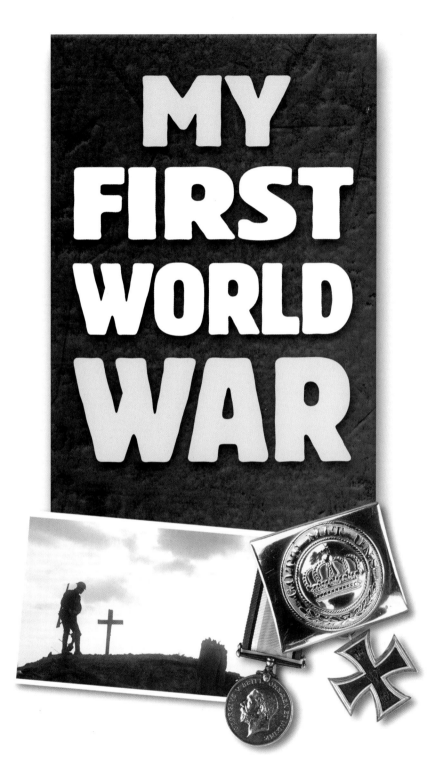

MY FIRST WORLD WAR

Daniel James

FRANKLIN WATTS
LONDON•SYDNEY

IN ASSOCIATION WITH

IMPERIAL WAR
MUSEUM

First published in 2009 by Franklin Watts

Copyright © 2009 Franklin Watts

Franklin Watts
338 Euston Road
London NW1 3BH

Franklin Watts Australia
Level 17/207 Kent Street
Sydney, NSW 2000

A CIP catalogue record for this book is available
from the British Library.

Dewey number: 941.083

ISBN 978 0 7496 7115 0

Printed in China

Franklin Watts is a division of Hachette Children's Books,
an Hachette UK company.

www.hachette.co.uk

Editor: Sarah Ridley
Design: Billin Design Solutions
Editor in Chief: John C. Miles
Art director: Jonathan Hair
Maps: Jason Billin

With many thanks to Terry Charman and the staff at the Imperial War Museum's Document, Sound
and Photograph Archives.

Picture credits:
All images copyright © Imperial War Museum unless otherwise stated.

Front cover, clockwise from top: Q002756, Q57615A, HU093514, Q005717, Q21184, Q006354, Q103294, PST002734.
Medals and artefacts: Christopher F Seidler/Steve Shott/Franklin Watts
Back cover, clockwise from top: Q002756, Q005717, HU093514, Q21184, Q103294, Q006354, PST002734.
Medals and artefacts: Christopher F Seidler/Steve Shott/Franklin Watts

Insides: p1, pp2-3 Q103294; p05 Q002756; p08t Q005717, b Q013325; p09t and b/g Q006284, b Q014996;
p10 HU068471; p11 Roger-Viollet/Getty Images; p12t, b IWM repro right; p13 and b/g Hulton Archive/Getty Images;
p14t PST002734, b Q042003; p15 and b/g Q060706; p16 HU 093514; p17 and b/g Q102925; p19t Neame/IWM, b and
b/g Q011718; p20-21 Q004593, p21 and b/g Q011718; Scrimgeour/IWM, b © IWM; p23 and b/g Q114867; p24 SP
000452; p25 and b/g Q070701; p26 SP000771; p27 (main) Q043227, (inset and b/g) Q079823; p28t Q058456, b and
b/g HO000016; p29 Q67902; p30 Q103334; p31t Jellicoe/IWM, b and b/g Q114833; p32 Q001108; p33t CO000198, b
and b/g Q079501; p34-5 CO002265; p35 CO002202; p36 Q006284; p37t and b/g Q006354, b Q003188; p38
CO003373; p39t Q011506, b and b/g Q009271; p40 and b/g Q031229; p41t Q014996, b Q002756; pp42-45 Q004593;
pp46-48 Q002756.

Contents

Introduction

By July 1914, a series of alliances had created two blocks of power in Europe – the Entente Powers, or Allies (Britain, France and Russia) and the Central Powers (including Germany and Austria-Hungary).

The assassination of the Archduke Franz Ferdinand of Austria, in Bosnia on 28 June 1914, suddenly brought these alliances into play as the nations of Europe took sides. The resulting conflict, which we now call the First World War, lasted for over four years and claimed more than 22 million lives.

This book is a collection of interviews with individuals who shaped and were shaped by the war. Its aim is to show the human side of some of the events that took place during the bloodiest war the world had yet seen.

I Over by Christmas! 1914

When the Austrian Archduke was assassinated, most people in Britain assumed it would be 'business as usual'. Even after Germany invaded Belgium and Britain joined the war, many continued to think it would last a couple of months at most. It was only when the initial war of movement on the Western Front – the Allied retreat, counter-attack and the 'race to the sea' – proved inconclusive, that people at home realised it would not be over by Christmas.

II Trench Deadlock 1915

By mid-1915 both sides were dug into an elaborate system of trenches throughout Belgium and France known as the Western Front. Both sides attempted to break through enemy lines by developing new weapons and tactics, but at a cost of thousands of lives.

Looking elsewhere for a breakthrough, the Allies launched the Gallipoli campaign against the Ottoman Empire. The campaign lasted almost a year and was a complete failure.

At sea, German U-boats (submarines) attacked all merchant shipping bound for Allied ports. This was an attempt to starve Britain out of the war, but it also risked bringing the USA into it on the Allied side.

III Total War 1916

In 1916, Britain introduced conscription to increase the size of its army. Air operations started to play a significant part in the war from 1916 onwards, but the year saw the largest naval battle of the war (Jutland) and the first horrific Battle of the Somme, in which tens of thousands of men were killed.

IV Mutiny and Desertion 1917

With deadlock on the Western Front continuing into 1917, morale became a major factor as mutiny and desertion on all sides increased. The introduction of tanks by the British led to temporary gains at Cambrai, but nothing decisive. When two revolutions effectively took Russia out of the war, the Central Powers now had a temporary numerical advantage.

V Allied Victory? 1918

On 6 April 1917 America joined the war, but it took a year for its war effort to be fully mobilised. Germany had time for one more offensive, in Spring 1918. This pushed the Allies back in some cases to where they had been at the beginning of the war. The Germans had over-extended themselves, however, and were cut off from their supply lines. A combination of British land victories, American political influence and German war-weariness forced Germany to surrender.

The Allies made Germany sign the Treaty of Versailles, which blamed the Germans for the war and forced them to pay huge reparations.

The harsh terms of the treaty contributed to the rise of German nationalism and the outbreak of the Second World War, 20 years later.

Arch Assassin

The German Kaiser (Emperor) – on horseback at a military event before the start of the war.

The Austrian Archduke Franz Ferdinand was on a state visit to Sarajevo in Bosnia on 28 June 1914 when he was killed by a Bosnian assassin. Austria-Hungary blamed Serbia for the death and tensions quickly mounted between the two countries. But not everyone believed a full-blown European war was inevitable.

The German schoolboy: Walter Rapport was on a family outing when the Archduke was assassinated. He remembers:

> The assassination of the Austrian Archduke Franz Ferdinand took place on 28 June 1914, the day of the German Derby in Hamburg. It was the first time my parents took me to the races and a short time before the Derby, the music broke off – the orchestra stopped. A little later we got to know of the assassination in Sarajevo. And after we came home, my father had a conversation with the director of the Hamburg railway who lived next door to us and said, 'What would that all mean?' And they were both... very pessimistic.

The English schoolboy: Harold Bing was at school in 1914. He recalls:

> Public opinion felt this was a continental quarrel about the assassination of an Austrian Prince at Sarajevo. It had nothing to do with us and we needn't get involved. After Britain went to war, the *Daily Mail* had posters out with the slogan 'Business as Usual'.

The French student: Robert Poustis was taught about France's claim to the German-occupied territory of Alsace-Lorraine, another cause of tension in Europe:

> When I was a boy, in school and in the family, we often spoke about the lost provinces – Alsace-Lorraine, which had been stolen from France after the war of 1870. In the schools, the lost provinces were marked in a special colour on all the maps, as if we were mourning for them. We wanted to get them back.

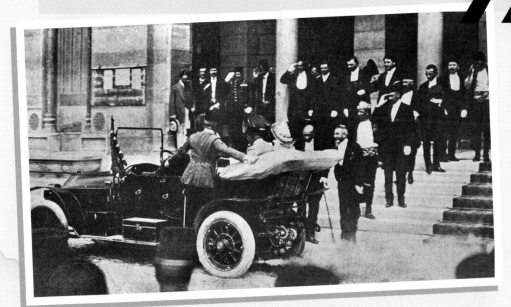

Archduke Franz Ferdinand and his wife, Sophie, get into a motor car to depart from the City Hall, Sarajevo, shortly before they were assassinated by the Bosnian Serb nationalist Gavrilo Princip on 28 June 1914.

The Austrian schoolboy: G D Lagus was still at school when the assassination occurred. He relates:

> We were lucky to have a master who taught us modern history, who was always implying that one day, under some pretext, the Austro-Hungarian monarchy would go to war with Serbia, which of course led all of us immediately to realise that this shot, most probably, will mean war.

The run up to war

Austria-Hungary gave Serbia an ultimatum, which they expected Serbia to reject. Before Serbia did so, Austria-Hungary looked for Germany's support in preparation for war.

Declarations of War

Once Austria-Hungary knew they could rely on Germany's support, they declared war on Serbia. The system of alliances, (made fun of in the cartoon, right), which had helped to keep the peace in Europe, now escalated the conflict. One by one the European powers were brought into the war.

The Briton abroad: Captain C J Chabot was living in Bangkok, Siam (now Thailand). He remembers people talking about the trouble in the Balkans but war was far from their thoughts.

The European population of Bangkok at this time was absolutely minimal, but nevertheless we had enough English people to rake up a rugby football team. This season the Germans had got an extraordinarily good team and as a final game of the season the Germans had challenged 'The Rest' and this was to be followed by dinner at the German Club. And so we duly played this game and we were duly beaten, and we duly congregated for the party at the German Club.

A bang at the door and a runner from the French Legation entered – with the extraordinary news of the outbreak of war and he was very quickly followed by another runner – the German. We didn't know what we ought to do, whether we ought to seize a knife off the table and plunge it into the next chap or what, but after a little bit of discussion, we decided that as far as we were concerned the war was going to start tomorrow and it wasn't going to start tonight, and the party proceeded and that was that.

The anti-war lobby: Harold Bing was still at school in 1914. He recalls:

> When I heard that a big anti-war demonstration was to be held in Trafalgar Square on Sunday the 2nd of August 1914 and Keir Hardie (the anti-war Labour politician) was to be one of the speakers, I walked from my home up to Trafalgar Square – about eleven miles [17.5 km] – took part in that demonstration, listened to Keir Hardie and of course walked home again afterwards, which perhaps showed a certain amount of boyish enthusiasm for the anti-war cause. It was quite a thrilling meeting with about ten thousand people.

Keir Hardie speaks in Trafalgar Square.

War declared

On 4 August 1914, Britain declared war on Germany, which was already at war with France and Russia. British Empire countries joined the Allies at once, but the USA remained neutral. Both sides expected a short and victorious resolution to the conflict.

Juining the Army

In 1914, Britain was the only major power not to have conscription, relying on volunteers for its army. It was heavily outnumbered by the other major European powers and on 7 August, the war minister, Lord Kitchener, began a recruitment drive.

BRITONS

"WANTS YOU"

JOIN YOUR COUNTRY'S ARMY!
GOD SAVE THE KING

Reproduced by permission of LONDON OPINION

The recruit: Thomas McIndoe was one of the young men who was caught up in the rush to enlist. He explains how he came to join the army:

> Well, I was always a tall and fairly fit lad and seeing the picture of Kitchener and his finger pointing, from any position you took up, the finger was always pointing at you…
>
> I resigned my job and went to the recruiting office at Arlsden. There was all types of men, from young lads to middle-aged men of forty, forty-five. But when I confronted the recruiting officer he said that I was too young, although I'd said that I was eighteen years of age.
>
> I returned home. And I picked up my bowler hat which my mother had bought me, which was only to wear on Sundays. And I donned that, thinking that it would make me look older. And I presented myself to the recruiting office again. This time no queries and I was accepted… I was sixteen in the June as the war broke out in the August.

Long queues formed at recruiting offices in September 1914.

New recruits

The recruiting campaign began well. By the end of September, more than half a million men had volunteered and there was no immediate need for conscription.

Belgium

A squadron of cavalry on the move.

After landing in France, the British Expeditionary Force (BEF) first engaged the Germans at the Battle of Mons, a town in the south-west of Belgium. The battle was fought by horse-mounted cavalry, infantry and artillery units.

The gunner: Gunner Walter Burchmore was in the Royal Horse Artillery, part of the BEF. He remembers the advance towards the Germans:

> We came into action on the high ground overlooking Mons. We immediately engaged the German artillery and that developed into a regular artillery duel in and around Binche, where we were firing in support of our infantry and cavalry. The infantry during the afternoon were driven out of Binche by sheer weight of numbers.
>
> Then developed quite a number of charges and counter-charges. We gave them all the support we could with our guns. We dealt very severely with a squadron of German cavalry who'd appeared on our right. We suddenly saw these people coming, didn't realise who they were at first, and said, 'By Crikey! It's bloody Germans!' so we started gunfire immediately. They wheeled away to the left and rode right into a squadron of our own cavalry who finished where we'd left off.
>
> The battle went on for several hours. We were very disappointed when we were ordered to break up the battle and retreat.
>
> As we withdrew we looked after ourselves by fighting about a dozen rearguard actions until we reached Landrecies... then fought another rearguard action all the way to Le Cateau. There we supported the 2nd Corps with our guns.

Forced to retreat

The Battle of Mons was a tactical victory for the British as they held the German advance off long enough to regroup. But the British were outnumbered and so were forced to retreat south.

15

The Great Retreat

During the 320-kilometre retreat from Mons to the River Marne, half the British force stopped and fought at Le Cateau on the night of 25 August, to give the rest a chance to get away.

The soldier: Private Charles Ditcham took part in the retreat with the 2nd Battalion, Argyll and Sutherland Highlanders.

> On the night of the 25th at one in the morning my battalion went into a factory in the village of Le Cateau. And at 4 o'clock we moved out hurriedly because the German Uhlans were at the other end of the village. So we took up our position to do a rearguard action for the Expeditionary Force. All this meant was that the company was put in a cornfield and we were told to dig ourselves in. So we just made a bit of a hole in the ground with our trenching tools and then took up position. Then the party started when the Hun came along. It was what made me realise what war was all about.
>
> We just lined up in the cornfield, one company on the right, one company on the left and these Germans came in their hordes and were just shot down.
>
> But they still kept coming and there were sufficient of them to shove us out of the field eventually. Afterwards, according to later accounts, it was an orderly retreat. Well, as one who took part in the orderly retreat, I didn't think it was very orderly.

Retreat
Of the 40,000 British soldiers fighting at Le Cateau, almost 8,000 were killed, injured or taken prisoner. The Allies continued the retreat to Saint Quentin.

An officer in the uniform of Argyll and Sutherland Highlanders. Steel helmets weren't introduced on the Western Front until 1916.

The Allied Counter-Attack

After the Battle of Saint Quentin, which bought more time for their retreat, the Allies dug in by the River Marne and prepared to make a last stand to defend Paris. The Germans were too exhausted and over-stretched to press home their advantage and, in September, the French led an Allied counter-attack, driving the Germans back over the rivers Marne and Aisne in two successive battles.

The sergeant: Sergeant Thomas Painting was in the 1st Battalion, King's Royal Rifle Corps. He describes his part in both battles:

> We went forward as we had been trained – one section would advance under covering fire of another section, leap-frogging each other as the others were firing to keep Jerrys' heads down. My company was going in with their bayonets when suddenly Jerry put up a white flag. We were really surprised. We took four hundred and fifty prisoners. I said to one of them, 'Why did you pack up when you've got so much ammunition?' He said, 'Well, your fire was so accurate we couldn't put our heads up to shoot at you.'
>
> At the Battle of the Aisne we got over the river and onto the high ground over a mile [about 2 km] in front of the Aisne. We knew there was about a brigade of Jerries against us and we were only seven platoons.
>
> During the fight we got pushed back about three hundred yards [275 m], we had to leave our wounded and dead. Private Wilson of the Highland Light Infantry and one of our men attacked a machine gun. Our man got killed, but Private Wilson killed the machine-gunner and captured the position and got the Victoria Cross. Our man got a wooden cross. That's the difference you see – one killed, one a Victoria Cross.

Dead lie on the battlefield.

Retreat and counter-attack

After the Great Retreat and the Allied counter-attack, the two sides became involved in a series of attempts to outflank each other to the north.

17

The Race to the Sea

From late September to mid-October, each side tried to outflank the other to the north to cut off their supply lines. This resulted in a race northwards, which later became known as the 'Race to the Sea'.

Trench survivor: Archibald James served on the Western Front in 1914 with the 3rd Hussars.

> We were constantly employed as dismounted cavalry to take over trench lines, usually for a short time before infantry became available. The British front had been extended to the north. And the line in the north of Flanders was held mainly by old French territorials. The trenches were very sketchy. And we were quite ill-adapted to this sort of work and quite unsuitably clothed for it. As indeed at that stage of the war were the infantry for trench warfare.
>
> The worst episode was three miserable days when we stood-to in the afternoon then rode about ten miles [16 km]. Then on the way it came on to pour with rain. And by the time we got to about a mile and a half [2.4 km] from the trenches we were to take over we were all absolutely soaked to the skin. We then handed over our horses and we marched up in the dark and took over the trenches.
>
> They had been constructed shortly before by French territorials. It was too wet to dig down and the parapet consisted largely of dead French bodies covered over with a superficial covering of earth. There was no wire in front of us. And the German trenches were about thirty yards [27 m] away.
>
> We had three days in these wretched little trenches, frozen miserable. And we had the greatest difficulty getting rations up because from one flank the Germans overlooked our rear. And when we got back to billets after three nights in these trenches, we had without exception what were afterwards known as 'trench feet'.

Trench deaths

As winter approached, life in the trenches took its toll on the troops. The army was ill-prepared for trench warfare and conditions often proved as deadly as enemy fire.

First Battle of Ypres

Ypres, just inside the Belgian border with northern France, was the last Allied stronghold before the Germans reached the Channel ports. The First Battle of Ypres took place from October to November. Both sides struggled to break through the trenches which always favoured the defending forces.

The engineer: Philip Neame was at Ypres. He was one of the first soldiers to improvise hand grenades, as he recalls:

> The Germans were very well supplied with very well made hand grenades and they started using them in trench warfare and we had no proper reply. Therefore we started devising home-made hand grenades which were called bombs and these were made out of empty used jam tins which were filled with rivets, hob-nails, any small bits of metal. And the explosive was usually two small bits of gun cotton with a detonator and the necessary bit of fuse projecting from the end of the jam tin.
>
> Trenches are all designed with traverses between each firebay with the purpose of preventing the enemy, if they capture a length of trench, preventing him shooting down the whole length of trench. You can't shoot the enemy in the next firebay – the only way of getting at him is by lobbing a hand grenade over the traverse into the next bay of the trench, and the hand grenade goes off with a terrific explosion and will probably kill or wound all the soldiers in that length of trench. That's the use of the hand grenade in trench warfare.

Entrenchment

The First Battle of Ypres lasted into November as the last reserves of the British Army just managed to hold off the Germans. The fighting eased off as the soldiers prepared for the first winter of the war.

A female worker inspects Mills hand grenades in a British factory during the First World War.

The Christmas Truce

As the first Christmas approached, it became clear that the war was not going to be over any time soon. In some places along the Western Front, Christmas Day provided a day's relief from the fighting and a chance for the troops to rest, relax a little and bury their dead. Some even met the men they had been trying so hard to kill.

The soldier: Private Frank Sumpter was in the London Rifle Brigade. He recalls the unofficial truce:

> After the 19th December attack, we were back in the same trenches when Christmas Day came along. It was a terrible winter, everything was covered in snow, everything was white. The devastated landscape looked terrible in its true colours – clay and mud and broken brick – but when it was covered in snow, it was beautiful. Then we heard the Germans singing, 'Silent Night, Holy Night', and they put up a notice saying 'Merry Christmas', so we put one up too.
>
> While they were singing our boys said, 'Let's join in,' so we joined in and when we started singing, they stopped. And when we stopped, they started again. So we were easing the way. Then one German took a chance and jumped up on top of the trench and shouted out, 'Happy Christmas, Tommy!' So of course our boys said, 'If he can do it, we can do it,' and we all jumped up. A sergeant-major shouted, 'Get down!' but we said, 'Shut up Sergeant, it's Christmas time!' And we all went forward to the barbed wire.

We could barely reach through the wire, because the barbed wire was not just one fence, it was two or three fences together, with a wire in between.

And so we just shook hands and I had the experience of talking to one German who said to me, 'Do you know where the Essex Road in London is?' I replied, 'Yes, my uncle had a shoe repairing shop there.' He said, 'That's funny. There's a barber shop on the other side where I used to work.' It's ironic when you think about it, that he must have shaved my uncle's head at times and yet my bullet might have found him and his bullet might have found me.

Participants in the Christmas Truce pose for the camera.

The truce ends

Officers were seriously concerned that they would lose control of their men, so they ordered them to return to their trenches. The truce did not last and fighting resumed in time for New Year.

Gas Attack

The only major assault by the Germans on the Western Front in 1915 was the Second Battle of Ypres, where they used poison gas against the Allies for the first time. At 5 pm on 22 April, Allied troops noticed a greenish-yellow cloud heading towards them. Thinking it was merely a smokescreen, Allied troops were ordered to take up their firing positions and open fire on the expected German advance.

Captain Scrimgeour, who is credited with the idea of how to counter-act the poison gas that Private Bromfield mentions.

The survivor: Private Alfred Bromfield of the 2nd Battalion, East Lancashire Regiment was at the battle.

> The 22 April is a day I shall always remember. I was standing in the trench cooking my breakfast. It was my chief interest in those days and I was very fond of fried bacon and cheese. I'd already made a drop of tea in my dixie so I took the lid and put in a couple of slices of bacon that I'd been saving and fried it up. I used to lay that on a slice of bread, then chop my cheese up very fine and drop it into the bacon fat with a drop of water so it wouldn't stick. I fried it up till it was bubbling then turned it out, onto the bacon and bread, and it was just like a hot cream cheese.
>
> Anyway I was getting on with that when one of our chaps on lookout yelled, 'Cor, look at the lyddite shells bursting along Jerry's trench.' Lyddite wasn't used a great deal so we jumped up out of curiosity to see these shells bursting along the trench. We watched a dozen puffs of yellow smoke coming up until we lost interest and got down into the trench again. About six seconds later the lookout yelled, 'Blimey, it's not lyddite, it's gas!' The officer came running out and gave the order, 'Open immediate rapid fire!'
>
> The gas had reached us and we had no protection at all beyond our own inventiveness – there were no such things as gas masks or pads in those days. We'd been tipped off that the only way to protect ourselves was by urinating on our handkerchiefs and covering our mouths with them. So we did that for long enough to get a good deep breath, then continued firing. That's how it went on while all the time the gas was still pouring over the top of the trench.

Aftermath of a gas attack.

The witness: Private W A Quinton was in the trenches. He describes the effects of chlorine gas:

> The men came tumbling over from the front line. I've never seen so many men so terror-stricken, they were tearing at their throats and their eyes were glaring out. Blood was streaming from those who were wounded and they were tumbling over one another. Those who fell couldn't get up because of the panic of the men following them, and eventually they were piled up two or three high in this trench.
>
> One chap had his hand blown off and his wrist was fumbling around, tearing at his throat. In fact it was the most gruesome sight I'd seen in the war. We manned the firing step, thinking the Germans would be on their way over, but strangely enough they didn't attack us.

Poison gas victims, with damaged lungs, lie on stretchers outside a hospital.

Horrible results

Almost 6,000 French and colonial troops died within ten minutes of the gas being released. Many survivors abandoned their posts in terror and a large gap was opened up in the Allied front line. However, the Germans had not expected such effective results and did not have enough men in the area to exploit the gap. Canadian troops were brought in as reinforcements and the gap in the line was closed. Both sides set to work on finding better ways to use and defend against chlorine gas and other chemical weapons.

Gallipoli

With the Western Front in deadlock, the Allies decided to attack the Ottoman Empire, which had joined the Central Powers in October 1914. It was decided to launch a naval attack on the Dardanelles, the tactically important stretch of water belonging to the Turks, separating the Balkans of Europe from Asia Minor.

The campaign began in February with naval bombardments of the Turkish fortresses on the hills, followed by landings at the end of April. The Allies eventually got ashore, but spent the rest of the year in trench deadlock and deteriorating conditions.

SS River Clyde was run aground at Cape Helles as close as possible to the shore so that the troops could disembark.

The soldier: Fusilier W Flynn of the 1st Battalion, Royal Munster Fusiliers was involved in various stages of the Gallipoli campaign. He recalls:

> When we woke up on the SS *River Clyde* in the morning and saw land, they told us it was the Dardanelles and we had to make a landing there. It was Cape Helles. All we could see was this piece of land shaped like a saucer which gradually went up to a little hill, which dominated the whole beach.
>
> Our cue was when the Dublins came off the warship in cutters. We then had to run down the gangway across the two boats and a steam hopper, then we only had 10 or 20 feet to go to the shore. But the boat had been carried away towards a strip of rock, and the steam hopper and one of the lighters [open boat] had been cut away and drifted out to sea...
>
> Anyway, we managed to scramble on the shore and we got behind a bank about five feet high, where we were safe for the time being.
>
> We made another big advance on the 29th and got right to the bottom of the whole trouble – that was Achi Baba, which dominated the whole peninsula right out to sea. It was a tidy-sized hill. We had lost a lot of men in

the trench fighting and then we had the order to retire, what was left of us. There was just one man here, perhaps two another twenty yards away, and we had to retire right down to the narrowest part. General Ian Hamilton promised reinforcements if we got ashore within a fortnight, but it was more than six weeks before we got any...

We did get black towards the end. We weren't succeeding at all, all we were doing was losing a lot of men and ships. Every day we were bringing in different men, different faces, all tired, all beaten. And it was so hot that summer, so hot. Then, as autumn came on, we were watching a picture of failure fought out by brave men.

When we withdrew on the 20 December it was dark. The soldiers were all packed so tight and quiet in the barges making their way to the big ships. We never lost a man, which was remarkable. As we were steaming quietly away, I thought of what 'Pincher' Martin had said to me a few days after we'd arrived at Sulva Bay: 'We're not going to be flying the Union Jack here.' He was right. We were never going to make it ours.

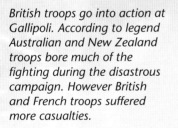

British troops go into action at Gallipoli. According to legend Australian and New Zealand troops bore much of the fighting during the disastrous campaign. However British and French troops suffered more casualties.

A disaster

The Gallipoli campaign was a disaster with more than 200,000 Allied casualties. Those responsible, including Winston Churchill, who had been deeply involved as First Lord of the Admiralty, were forced to resign or were replaced as the Allies withdrew at the end of the year.

U-boats and the *Lusitania*

Germany reduced the flow of food and supplies to Britain by using U-boats to attack merchant ships as they crossed the Atlantic. The legality of this type of warfare was disputed throughout the war and it severely strained relations between Germany and the USA.

The submariner: Edgar von Spiegel spent much of the war in a German U-boat (the photo below shows an example captured by Britain).

Life on the submarine? It depends much on the size and type. In the old submarines the crew was packed like sardines in a box. It depends also very much on the conditions – whether calm or stormy weather. Submarines have terrible hard and short shaking movements which are hard to bear for the crew. But in wartime certainly we didn't mind the life on the boat so much because we had other goals. We had to fight.

After the blockade of Germany, the German government decided to fight this blockade with submarine war against merchant ships. We got orders and counter orders all the time during the first period, 1914, 1915, 1916. The unrestricted submarine war only really began in 1917, 1 February.

We didn't like that business very much, we submarine men, because we were seamen, we didn't like to sink ships, which we loved... And the result of these damn torpedoes were certainly very often heart-breaking. I remember one which got the torpedo in the bow and went down, slipped down, like an aeroplane. In two minutes the ten-thousand tonne ship had disappeared from the surface.

There was one very dreadful and terrible accident during the first war, 1915, when one of the huge Cunard liners, the *Lusitania*, was sunk.

After the Lusitania, *above, was sunk by a German U-boat, the British government used the outrage felt by the general public to encourage people to enlist, as seen in the poster, right.*

The commander of the submarine who sunk the *Lusitania*, Captain Schwieger, was a great friend of mine, he was a wonderful man, he couldn't kill a fly and still, he caused this very terrible disaster. It was not his fault.

There were three huge Cunard liners as far as I remember – the *Aquitania*, the *Mauretania*, the *Lusitania*. They were all over 45,000 tonnes in size, four funnels and they were in the colours of the Cunard liners...

Now when this submarine saw this huge ship coming, the captain certainly saw it and had to think it was a (military) transport ship not a liner... he would have acted against his duty if he had not fired his torpedoes.

"

The legacy of the U-boat sinkings

The sinking of the *Lusitania* provoked outcry in Britain and the USA. The liner sank so quickly that over half of its 2,000 passengers and crew drowned, including 128 US citizens. After the 1917 announcement of unrestricted submarine warfare, the Germans managed to sink roughly a quarter of the shipping, regardless of nationality, entering the area around the British Isles. Britain responded by introducing escorted convoys, which were partially successful, but U-boats remained one of the greatest threats to Britain's survival during the war. The sinking of American ships by U-boats was one of the reasons why the USA eventually declared war on Germany in 1917.

The War in the Air

The German Zeppelin L13.

In 1915 Germany attacked London from the air using airships, sometimes called zeppelins, or zepps, to drop bombs.

The munitions worker: Lilian Mary Bineham was at work when an air raid occurred. She recalls:

> It was just before we were knocking off, quarter past seven in the evening and we hear this awful explosion. Of course naturally we thought it was the Arsenal that had gone up, because the Arsenal was on this side of the river and Canning Town the other, just across the river which is not very wide, and ooh it was awful. We stopped for nothing, we didn't stop for outdoor clothes or anything. We just rushed to the gates all along the Woolwich Road, home. All in our magazine clothes.
>
> Bang after bang went and all along the river there was all these flames the other side of the river, the back of the Arsenal. It was this zepp that came over, I think it was the 101 it was called. And we saw it and we caught it – the flak on Blackheath guns – caught it. Ooh, it was a sight!
> As the flames died out you could see all the framework of the zepp itself – it was like a lot of lace – and you could see the bodies dropping, because they hold a lot those zepps you see. They were all Germans. And ooh, it was a marvellous sight, although it was sad.

The aftermath of a zeppelin raid in an English street.

Early in the war, aircraft were only used for observation purposes. In 1915, in order to deter similar observation missions by the enemy and to protect their own missions, the British started to send aeroplanes with guns into the skies.

The pilot: Frederick Winterbotham served with the Royal Flying Corps on the Western Front in 1917. He recalls a mission to escort and protect photographic reconnaissance aircraft over German lines:

"Well, the time came and suddenly there was an enormous barrage of anti-aircraft fire between us and the photographic machines. Now this was a new trick by the Germans, I couldn't see what the machines below me were doing. And at the same moment we were attacked, of course, out of the sun, by about a dozen German fighters. And we had a hell of a scrap. And after the first three minutes, my gun on the top of my plane jammed. There I was now without a gun. And you know what one was supposed to do? One was supposed to haul your gun down, off the top of the plane on its hinges, steer your aeroplane in the middle of a dogfight with your knees, and put your gun right and put it up again so that it fired again. I mean that was supposed to be the drill. Quite impossible anyway.

During the time that I was trying to clear the stoppage in my gun, somebody got on my tail... my engine just went 'phut' like that. So I was then left in an aeroplane in the middle of a dogfight without a gun and without an engine. We were so far over the German line, absolutely hopeless to try and get back again. Any case, I had to start going down...

I eventually went nose first into a shell hole and the aeroplane turned upside-down. I got my head jammed between the top wing and my nose was broken. I pulled myself out. I was terrified of fire. And as I crawled out from this shattered aeroplane I found myself surrounded by German soldiers, all pointing their rifles at me."

British Sopwith Camel fighter aircraft.

The role of aircraft

Aircraft played a smaller part in the First World War compared to future wars. Nevertheless, during the war, they became specialised into fighters, bombers and observation aircraft and in 1918 the Royal Air Force (RAF) became a separate branch of the armed forces in its own right.

Conscription

With recruitment numbers falling off badly towards the end of 1915, the government was forced to consider conscription. Politicians knew this would not be popular, so they decided to introduce it bit by bit. The first Military Service Act in January 1916 conscripted only unmarried men between the ages of 18 and 40. However, not everyone believed conscription was right. Pacifists refused to fight and became known as conscientious objectors (lampooned in the cartoon, above).

The conscientious objector: Harold Bing refused to serve in the armed forces, despite conscription. He wrote:

> Well, when the act was published and the date was fixed by which applications for exemption on any ground – health, business, conscientious objection or anything else – was fixed, I sent in my application to the local tribunal and in due course I was summoned to appear before it. The hearing was rather a farce. When my name was called I appeared before the tribunal, I had my father and two other friends there to speak as witnesses on my behalf. The chairman of the tribunal, after one or two formal questions, asked me how old I was. I said I was eighteen years of age. He said, 'Oh – in that case you're not old enough to have a conscience. Case dismissed!' My father got up to protest at such summary treatment, but the chairman called, 'Next case, next case.' The clerk explained that there was no next case, I was the last case that day, so the chairman and fellow members of the tribunal got up and left the room, leaving my father still protesting.

Conscription arrives

Conscientious objectors worked on farms or alongside soldiers, as medical orderlies. Those who came before a military tribunal, including Harold Bing, spent up to three years in prison. The First Military Service Bill was one of the most important laws passed in Britain during the war. At a time when numbers of new recruits were falling, conscription kicked in just in time to replenish the decimated army after the costly battles of the summer of 1916.

Jutland

The Battle of Jutland was the largest naval battle of the war. It was fought between the Grand Fleet of the Royal Navy and the High Seas Fleet of the Imperial German Navy in the North Sea near Jutland, Denmark.

The gunner: Captain Grant was on the HMS *Lion* during the Battle of Jutland. His job was to ensure the supply of ammunition to the turret guns on board.

> I then made for Q [turret] which was in the centre of the ship... To get to Q one had to descend into a small flat where a first aid and electric light party was stationed, and then down into the handling room. Here everyone was standing about in silence. When I asked what was the matter, the Sergeant in charge said that something had gone wrong in the turret and that the Major in charge of the turret had ordered the magazines to be flooded [to prevent them exploding]... It was also reported that the supply cages were full. It would therefore appear that there was outside the magazine at least two full charges in the supply cages and there may have been two more in the loading cages in the working chamber which was immediately under the guns.
>
> While I was making these inquiries, men from the working chamber were coming down the trunk into the handing room. I asked them what had happened and they informed me that a shell had pierced the turret, exploding inside, killing the gun's crew, and that the turret was completely out of action. Q turret was manned by the Royal Marines, with Major Harvey in charge. Major Harvey, although lying mortally wounded, to his everlasting glory thought of the safety of the ship and ordered the magazines to be flooded. For this gallant deed in safeguarding the ship he was posthumously awarded the Victoria Cross.

Tactical victory

Although Britain lost 6,000 sailors to Germany's 2,500, Britain claimed victory as Germany did not risk her fleet in such an open battle again during the war.

HMS Warspite *and* Malaya *seen from HMS* Valiant *during the Battle of Jutland.*

The Somme

The Battle of the Somme began on 1 July 1916 after 18 months of trench deadlock. The aim was to relieve pressure on the French troops at Verdun.

The captain: Captain Alfred Irwin fought at the Battle of the Somme. He recounts:

> We had a lot of warning that the Battle of the Somme was coming. I'm quite certain the Boche knew. If he hadn't, the barrage would have told him. For the two or three days before the Somme it was intensive, in order to break up the wire in front of the front line. I took it for granted that the wire would be cut, that we'd massacre the Boche in their front line, get to our objectives and then be sent to do something else next day.
>
> Captain Neville was commanding one of our two assaulting companies. And a few days before the Battle of the Somme he came to me with a suggestion – that as he and his men were all equally ignorant of what their conduct would be when they got into action, he thought it might be helpful as he had 400 yards to go and knew that it would be covered by machine gun fire, it would be helpful if he could furnish each platoon with a football and allow them to kick it forward and follow it.
>
>
>
> And I sanctioned that on condition that he and his officers really kept command of the units and didn't allow it to develop into a rush after the ball.
>
> They went forward shouting with such energy, kicking the football ahead of them. But so quickly Neville and his second in command were both killed plus his company sergeant-major. I picked up all the chaps I could and went over the parapet and said, 'Come on' and they came quite smoothly.
>
> Eventually we reached the German third reserve line. We were so lamentably few that there was very little we could do. We'd come down from 800 men to something under 200 in that attack, and it seemed to me a dreadful waste of life. All my best chaps had gone.

The soldier poet: Walter Hird wrote a poem about his terrible experiences at the Somme in 1917.

Casualties of the battle rest outside a field hospital.

> *In the bloody battle of the Somme through hell,*
> *How could your kingdom come?*
> *Behind the German lines we see*
> *What used to be*
> *The thousands killed by shot and shell*
> *We laid on them we lived in hell*
> *The stink of water, blood and slime*
> *Spoke through the clothes of pals of mine*
> *As on each one, we used to tread*
> *We often wished that we were dead*
> *If hell was never known before*
> *'Twas there it cried encore encore*
> *Here men went forth to meet his maker*
> *Away from kin and undertaker*
> *Bundles in blankets of bodies rent*
> *Their souls away to heaven sent*
> *In tears we bore this bloody stall*
> *And prayed God save us from it all.*

A soldier carries a wounded comrade to safety in a trench at the Somme.

Huge death toll

The Battle of the Somme lasted for five months and was one of the most bitterly contested and costly battles of the First World War. Gains were minimal and human losses were huge.

Over a million men lost their lives in the course of the battle. On the first day alone, 20,000 British troops died.

Passchendaele

From July to November, the Third Battle of Ypres raged for control of the village of Passchendaele near the town of Ypres. The Allies planned to break through German lines and advance to the Belgian coast to capture the German submarine bases, which were crucial to the war at sea. After the disastrous Nivelle Offensive, the French forces were on the brink of mutiny and there was a real danger that British morale would collapse too.

The artillery officer: Bombardier J W Palmer of the 26th Brigade, Royal Field Artillery, wrote of the mental and physical struggle to survive Passchendaele.

> It was mud, mud, everywhere: mud in the trenches, mud in front of the trenches, mud behind the trenches. Every shell hole was a sea of filthy, oozing mud. I suppose there's a limit to everything, but the mud of Passchendaele – to see men sinking into the slime, dying in the slime – I think it absolutely finished me off.
>
> I thought I was going to get killed. Every time I went out to mend the [telegraph] wire I think I was the biggest coward on God's earth. Nobody knew when a wire would go, but we knew that it had to be mended. The infantrymen's lives depended on those wires working. It didn't matter whether or not we'd had any sleep, we just had to keep those wires going.
>
> I hadn't had any sleep rest, it seemed, for weeks. It was very, very difficult to mend a telephone wire in this mud. You'd find one end and then you'd try to trudge through the mud to find the other end, but as you got one foot out the other one would sink down again.
>
> It was somewhere near midnight. The Germans were sending over quite a barrage and I crouched down in one of these dirty shell holes. I began to

think of those poor devils who'd been punished for self-inflicted wounds – some had even been shot.

I began to wonder if I could get out of it. I sat there and kept thinking. It's very lonely when you're on your own. Then in the distance I heard the rattle of a harness. I knew there were ammunition wagons coming up and I thought, 'Well, here's a way out – when they get level with me I'll ease out and put my leg under the wheel and I can plead it was an accident.'

I waited as the sound of the harness got nearer and nearer. Eventually I saw the leading horses' heads in front of me and I thought, 'This is it!' and began to ease my way out as the first wagon reached me. But you know, I never even had the guts to do it, I just couldn't do it. I think I was broken in spirit and mind.

"

Stretcher-bearers bringing in a wounded man over muddy ground at Passchendaele, 14 November 1917.

A disaster

Passchendaele is remembered both for the mud and for the 448,000 British and Empire troops who were killed and wounded there.

Cambrai

The Battle of Cambrai was the dawn of a new era in the history of warfare. The British used tanks effectively for the first time, but despite making significant inroads into enemy lines with their first assault, they failed to follow up or hold on to the ground that they had gained.

The tank officer: Norman Dillon served with the 2nd Battalion, Tank Corps on the Western Front.

" The location of the Battle of Cambrai was kept so secret that even my colonel didn't know about it. In fact, I was told before he was, because it was my job to reconnoitre the route. I planned the route in the usual way. We'd been allotted our frontage, so I knew where to go. It was about three miles, and I walked some of it during the day and the rest at dusk. I did my trick of laying a rope from the front line back over the route, dodging round things we wanted to avoid, and ending up where the tanks would start. I was pretty tired by the end of the day and got an hour of sleep.

On the night of the 20 November, we started moving tanks up to the starting position. The tanks were driven by relief drivers and crews to enable the crews to be fresh for battle. I was guiding them and I had a very nasty experience. I got caught up in some barbed wire. The leading tank was bearing down on me and I couldn't stop it or get free of the wire. I flashed my torch and held it up as high as I could, and the driver eventually stopped with a volley of oaths because it was an unheard-of thing to do. You should never flash a light at a driver because it blinds him. But that had been my purpose. I stopped the tank and got free.

This view of a British tank was taken from the bottom of a trench.

A tank tows a heavy field gun in the aftermath of Cambrai.

The trenches of the Hindenburg Line were our main objective. To cross that line with tanks was quite impossible, as it was enormously wide and deep. But the ingenuity of our HQ staff produced the answer. Enormous bundles of brushwood, about 5 feet in diameter, like enormous toilet rolls. They weighed about a tonne and a half and were carried on the nose of the tank. As the tank came to the trench, this bundle was released and fell into the bottom of the trench. This enabled the tank to nose down, rest on it, and crawl up over the other side, and in this way the uncrossable Hindenburg Line was crossed.

We got through all four German lines without any serious opposition. The tanks reached their objective quickly and when I caught up with them I found the crews sitting down drinking mugs of tea. The infantry were sculling about wondering at having got through so easily. If the cavalry corps had been on the spot to carry on the attack, as was intended, it could have been a major British victory. We could have pushed through to the other side of Cambrai and there would have been a complete readjustment of the German line. But the cavalry weren't produced until hours too late and then there weren't enough troops on the ground.

"

A positive result

Both sides lost just fewer than 50,000 men each but the German counter-attack meant that they regained their early losses and even advanced a little. Despite these statistics, the British took heart from the fact that a mixture of British tanks and ingenuity had managed to break through the strongest German trenches.

A group of German prisoners carry a wounded soldier on a stretcher.

Germany's Final Push

The USA joined the war in 1917, but it took almost a year before they could contribute significant numbers to the Western Front. When revolution took Russia out of the war in December, it freed up a million German soldiers from the Eastern Front to be redeployed to fight the Allies in the West. Germany had the numerical advantage and one last chance to end the war in their favour.

The sergeant-major: Richard Tobin was on the Western Front in 1918. He wrote:

> We took the line in the spring of 1918 – tough, grim and determined. We were hardened veterans of many battles. Our constitutions had survived the winter. The battalion wit said we were quality, not quantity. The collapse of Russia had released a huge German army.
>
> On 20 March my battalion was lying on the Cambrai front. We were brigade reserve, the front line was being bombarded. Mid-March soaked us with gas shells, thousands a day fell. Mustard gas had lain in the hollows for days and reduced the voice to a whisper. We were a whispering army. But we would go back foot by foot, inch by inch, fighting and killing.
>
> On 26 March we dropped into a trench. It was a trench we knew of old. We had started to retreat on 21 March, 1918, and here we were back in the trench we had started to attack from on 13 November 1916.

A patriotic swimmer holds US and British flags in the summer of 1918.

It was leap-frog in reverse. Battalion went through battalion. Company through company. And so we came back to the Somme battlefields and Field Marshal Haig's famous message: 'With our backs to the wall and believing in the justice of our cause.' No more retreating.

The only lead in our hearts was the thought that we were back to the old trench ding-dong. No signs of an end. So the weeks and months went by. April, May... We even did one or two small attacks.

When we were out of the line we used to stand by the road and watch the fresh, strong, plump and new American battalions swing by. They waved and laughed and shouted. Our boys grinned back. But we wondered, 'Did they know? Could they do it? Would they do it?'

In the summer of 1918 came the breakthrough. We had left the trenches behind, those mud-sodden trenches that we had hated for so many years. We were out in the open country. We almost felt victory in the air. Admittedly the Germans were standing and fighting here and there, but the breakthrough had come. It was open warfare. We were in green fields once again. The commander had to watch his flanks, wondering when to stop, when to dig in, when to go on. We also had our ration problems. But it looked like the end and the peace we had longed for.

Peace in sight

The Allied breakthrough had come. As the Allies advanced, the German people were on the brink of revolution. On 7 November, German commanders sued for peace to avoid the prospect of continuing the war on German soil.

Some of the thousands of German prisoners captured at the end of the war.

Armistice

The armistice treaty between the Allies and Germany was signed in a railway carriage in Compiègne Forest near Paris, France, and came into effect later that day – at 11 am (Paris time) on the 11th day of the 11th month of 1918. It was signed by Marshal Ferdinand Foch on behalf of the Allies and Matthias Erzberger for the Germans.

A military band leads a victory parade in Winchester to celebrate the Armistice.

The Australian officer: Major Keith Officer served in France.

He remembers the precise moment that the war ended:

> At 11 o'clock on the 11th of November, I was sitting in a room, in the brewer's house at Le Cateau, which had been Sir John French's headquarters at the time of the Battle of Mons. I was sitting at a table with a major in the Scots Greys who had a large, old-fashioned hunting watch, which he put on the table and watched the minutes going round. When 11 o'clock came, he shut his watch up and said, 'I wonder what we are all going to do next?' To some of us it was the end of four years, to others three years, to some, less. For many of us it was practically the only life we had known. We had started so young.
>
> Nearby there was a German machine-gun unit giving our troops a lot of trouble. They kept firing until precisely 11 o'clock. At precisely 11 o'clock, an officer stepped out of their position, stood up, lifted his helmet and bowed to the British troops. He then fell in all his troops in the front of the trench and marched them off. I always thought that this was a wonderful display of confidence in British chivalry, because the temptation to fire on them must have been very great.

The end of the war led to the Treaty of Versailles, which imposed huge penalties on Germany. This picture shows the treaty negotiations in 1919.

The British officer: Sergeant-Major Richard Tobin wrote about how he felt when the war finally ended.

> The Armistice came, the day we had dreamed of. The guns stopped, the fighting stopped. Four years of noise and bangs ended in silence. The killings had stopped.
>
> We were stunned. I had been out since 1914. I should have been happy. I was sad. I thought of the slaughter, the hardships, the waste and the friends I had lost.

War over

Nearly five years, four fallen empires and nearly ten million military deaths later, the First World War was over. The Armistice was soon cemented by the Treaty of Versailles. Ironically, the treaty is often viewed as causing many of the problems that led to the Second World War, 20 years later.

Symbol of the war: a lone British soldier stands by the grave of a fallen comrade.

Glossary

Allies Those who are on the same side as each other. In the First World War it refers to the Entente Powers – see entry.

Arsenal (Woolwich) A centre of weapons manufacture in London.

Artillery Large guns, such as cannons, or the branch of an army that specialises in using them.

Barrage Heavy artillery fire directed in front of friendly troops to screen them from the enemy.

Battalion A grouping in the army of around 850 men.

Bayonet A blade attached to a rifle and used in close combat.

Billet A resting place for soldiers.

Boche An offensive term for a German.

Bowler hat A hard, round, black hat with a rim, as worn by business men.

Brigade A group of regiments or battalions in the army.

Cavalry Soldiers trained to fight on horseback.

Central Powers The nations opposed to the Allies; Germany, Austria-Hungary and later the Ottoman Empire and Bulgaria.

Chemical weapons Weapons using the toxic properties of gas or other chemicals.

Colonial Belonging to a colony, a region under the control of a distant country.

Company A military unit, under the command of a captain and made up of at least two platoons or 120 men.

Conscription Compulsory enrolment in the armed forces.

Convoy An accompanying force, often of armed ships, escorting merchant ships.

Counter-attack A return attack.

Demonstration A rally, march or protest.

Desertion When an individual leaves the armed forces without permission.

Dixie A military cooking kettle.

Enfilading Penetrating with gunfire.

Entente Powers The nations opposed to the Central Powers; France, Russia, Britain and later Italy. The United States was an Associated Power from 1917.

Firebay Firebays were straight sections of trench where soldiers shot from whilst traverses were built at angles.

Flak Anti-aircraft artillery.

Fusiliers A regiment consisting of infantry who once fought with a special type of weapon called a flintlock musket.

Hindenburg Line A strong system of trench defences in north-eastern France constructed by the Germans in the winter of 1916-17.

Hun A nickname for German soldiers.

Infantry Soldiers who fight on foot.

Jerry A nickname for German soldiers.

Latrine Basic toilet.

Lyddite shell A form of high explosive.

Magazine Where ammunition is stored.

Mobilised/mobilisation To prepare armed forces for battle.

Munitions War material, especially weapons and ammunition.

Nationalism Devotion to the interests of one's nation.

Ottoman Empire A vast former empire centred around what is now Turkey that was dissolved after the First World War.

Platoon A subdivision of a company, usually commanded by a lieutenant.

Poison gas A gas used in warfare to kill. Chlorine gas is an example.

Race to the sea The name given to a period of mobile warfare on the Western Front from September to October 1914 when both sides tried to outflank each other in Belgium.

Reconnoitre To explore an area in order to gather military intelligence.

Recruiting officer An officer in charge of signing people up to the armed forces.

Reparations The compensation for war damage paid by a defeated state.

Squadron A cavalry or armoured unit of an army.

Stalemate A deadlock.

Territorials Members of the British Army reserves.

Treaty of Versailles The peace treaty that ended the First World War, signed on 28 June 1919, seven months after the Armistice had ended the fighting.

Trench foot An infection of the feet, caused by long-term exposure to damp socks and boots.

Truce A temporary end to hostilities.

U-boat A German submarine.

Uhlans A unit of cavalry that formed part of the German, Austrian and Russian armies.

Unrestricted submarine warfare A type of naval warfare in which submarines sink merchant ships without warning.

Victoria Cross Britain's highest military award for exceptional bravery.

Western Front The dividing line between the opposing sides in Europe – the trenches that ran from the Swiss border to the North Sea.

Zepp The shortened name for a zeppelin, a type of German airship.

Some useful websites

The Imperial War Museum's official website: www.iwm.org.uk

Encyclopedic site about the First World War: www.spartacus.schoolnet.co.uk/FWW.htm

BBC history site about the First World War: www.bbc.co.uk/history/worldwars/wwone/

Note to parents and teachers:
Every effort has been made by the Publishers to ensure that the websites in this book are suitable for children, that they are of the highest educational value, and that they contain no inappropriate or offensive material. However, because of the nature of the Internet, it is impossible to guarantee that the contents of these sites will not be altered. We strongly advise that Internet access is supervised by a responsible adult.

Index